EXPLORATIONS
OF A
COSMIC SOUL

ALLIE MICHELLE

Andrews McMeel
PUBLISHING®

EXPLORATIONS OF A COSMIC SOUL

Andrews McMeel Publishing
a division of Andrews McMeel Universal
1130 Walnut Street, Kansas City, Missouri 64106

www.andrewsmcmeel.com

21 22 23 24 25 BVG 10 9 8 7 6 5 4 3 2 1

ISBN: 978-1-5248-6812-3

Library of Congress Control Number: 2021932763

Editor: Patty Rice
Art Director: Tiffany Meairs
Production Editor: Jasmine Lim
Production Manager: Cliff Koehler

Cover illustration by Anfisa Kuzmina

ATTENTION: SCHOOLS AND BUSINESSES
Andrews McMeel books are available at quantity discounts with
bulk purchase for educational, business, or sales promotional use.
For information, please e-mail the Andrews McMeel Publishing
Special Sales Department: specialsales@amuniversal.com.

This book is the physical
manifestation of lessons learned
through the school of everyday life.

It is for the seeker.

It is for the one who chooses to dive
into unexplored depths.

It is for the one who is ready to meet the
truth within themselves.

It is for you.

May you connect to the universe inside.

Foreword

BY JILL WINTERSTEEN OF SPIRIT DAUGHTER
(ASTROLOGIST AND OVERALL MAGICAL HUMAN)

In the current transformative time both cosmically and earthly, we have been given a few shining stars—beacons of light to guide us on our journey. Allie Michelle is one of them. Her poetry and the energy it imbues provides a pathway from dark to light, from untruth to truth, and from destruction to nourishment. A path that parallels the movement of our stars and the story of the universe.

In the past six months, there has been a steady shift in energy in the collective consciousness, a changing of the guard, so to speak, and with that, we are witnessing the rise of the feminine energy. Feminine energy by this definition is one that heals, one that nourishes, one that is of service, and one that is powerful enough to give life to any area that needs it.

It has long been predicted by shamans, yoga masters, and spiritual teachers that women will heal this planet with their feminine energy. They will heal the earth from the destruction of war, they will heal society from its ego-driven insecurities, and they will heal our relationships with each other. What has been a long-standing prediction is now evidenced by the movement of the stars and the movement of the feminine voice.

In 2011, a star known as Regulus transitioned from Leo to Virgo. Regulus holds the energy of regality, leadership, and defense of these positions. For over 2000 years, Regulus was home to the lion constellation that formed his very heart. And over the last 600 years, Regulus was in the last third of Leo, which is ruled by Mars, the planet of war. No wonder so much blood has been shed, and whole societies were left heartbroken during this time. Where Leo represents masculine leadership, Virgo represents an empowered woman, self-sufficient and capable of great healing.

Regulus has shifted into the first part of Virgo ruled by Mercury, the planet of communication, and this energy is influencing the way both male and female leaders communicate with each other and their community. With Regulus entering Virgo, this kingly star is shifting from King to Queen and God to Goddess.

Kings rule by power, queens rule through service. They both have power—they both are rulers, leaders, and teachers—but their approach is very different. In August of 2017, we experienced an amazing total solar eclipse in the Northern Hemisphere, particularly in North America, which has been a leader in the feminine movement since the sixties. This eclipse took place within two degrees of Regulus, providing an energetic catalyst to the shifting energy from Leo to Virgo. The eclipse also occurred at the north node in Leo, which gave the transiting energy a pathway.

North nodes tell us where we are going—they outline our karmic path both individually and as a society. This combination of Regulus transitioning to Virgo combined with the north node still giving us direction through Leo teaches us leadership based in service. It is the energy of individual kingdoms with the intent of serving humanity as their mission. This energy will usher in leaders with unity and compassion at the heart of their decisions and will bring forth a feminine perspective of healing for all.

The solar eclipse opened a portal for us to step through, and on the other side, feminine energy is empowered, leading and healing our world. It's a process, though, and we've been witnessing it unfolding over the past few months. Feminine energy and the feminine voice have been suppressed for a long time, and their rising is bound to bring about some friction, some shadow work, and some drama.

When energy is subdued for a long period of time, its reemergence can be explosive. This emerging energy was given an extra push when Jupiter entered Scorpio in October of 2017, the same week the #MeToo movement started. Jupiter is the planet of expansion, while Scorpio is the underground, the shadow side, and a sign of hidden secrets.

When Jupiter met Scorpio's stars, combined with the already rising feminine, women all over joined as a community and expanded their voices and their hearts as they shared the hidden secrets within them. It was a necessary movement for the feminine to continue its awakening and its reclamation of power. The power that has always been hers to claim.

The rise of the feminine energy is preceded by the rise of the feminine voice, which will be fueled by a lunar eclipse in January and a solar eclipse in February. Both involve the energy of Aquarius, who is known for her outspokenness and ability to incite movement through her authentic voice.

At the time of this writing, these events have not occurred, but it is this writer's prediction that there are many more movements on the horizon, and women will become increasingly more outspoken about the fate of this planet. We will also see a rise in books like this one written by divine feminine leaders like Allie Michelle. They will inspire us and pass on heart-centered, healing messages through our communities. In May, there will be another energetic charge for the feminine, and that is Uranus moving into Taurus. Uranus is the planet of change, forward movement, and unknown shifts into new territory. He has been stationed in Aries for the last eight years, which is a highly masculine sign. Aries is known as the god of war and the planet of the self. Taurus, on the other hand, is very feminine in nature. She is an earth sign like Virgo and known for her love of art and the earth herself. She is the keeper of beauty and nature.

This transition from Aries to Taurus is much like the shifting of the star Regulus from Leo to Virgo. We are moving once again from self to community, from God to Goddess, and from destruction to nourishment. All governed by the planet of change, Uranus. This transit will push the rise of the feminine into a new gear, one that will usher in permanent change and transformation. We will begin to see more focus on the collective instead of the self, and we will lay down our ego-driven ways to help better the planet as a whole community.

Once again we will see the feminine energy developing steadily in each of us, men and women. A world ruled by feminine energy does not necessarily mean a world ruled solely by women. The feminine will rise in each gender, and men will learn to respect this part of themselves and let it guide them just like women have done for centuries.

So, what does a world dominated by feminine energy look like? When conflict arises, war will not be the only answer; new ways of negotiation will unfold. Nature herself will become more respected and made a priority in political agendas. There will be less ego involved in our countries' decisions, and service will become a priority. Women will become as powerful as men, and everyone will become equally respected no matter their ethnicities. New methods and paradigms will emerge in the way children are raised with both parents equally involved.

The stars are predicting not a role reversal per se but a new way of doing things that have not been explored. It will be the true age of Aquarius—cutting edge, progressive, and with the heart of humanity at its center. This is what a feminine future looks like. Most importantly, women will remain feminine. They will keep and highlight their femininity, treasuring it as we treasure the energy of Virgo and Taurus. Their intuition will no longer be questioned and beaten down by logic. It, along with all their emotions, will be praised and used as guidance, not something to medicate or see as a burden. Women are different than men; their brains work differently, and that difference is what the world needs. This difference is what will restore balance, and at the end of the day, that is what's occurring—the restoration of balance.

The following poetry is part of the restoration. It is feminine; it is born from intuition and emotion, it is beautiful. It inspires you to feel and reminds you that there is light in the world. The world may get a bit darker before we see the true emergence of light, but this book is a reminder that it is already here and balance is returning. Love, as you will read in this book, spreads like wildfire and won't take long before it drives out hatred. As you read these poems, let them remind you of the beauty in the world—feel them tap you into your feminine energy and inspire you to always lead with your heart.

Universal purpose :

I wrote this during my two week meditation course in the Himalayan Mountains. I went there expecting what many people do - an Eat Pray Love journey, or to return as some variation of yoda. Life has a cosmic sense of humor like that, because the complete opposite happened. We sat there meditating for 6-9 hours each day until all I felt was frustration and a sore back. It stormed for two weeks with hail the size of my fist, as though mother nature herself were pressing me inwards. And yet, everything that normally made up my identity, that i had feared losing, ceased to matter. The most fulfilled I've ever felt was sitting in stillness on those musty wooden floors, truly needing nothing but my own breath. And that's a lesson I'll always carry - the opportunity for fulfillment comes with simply being intimate with the moment.

Universal Purpose

What is your purpose?
What is your task?
To live, to love,
To show up for what the moment asks
Living is quite simple, you see
We are conscious agents here to Be
You want to change the world?
Then find what you love, and let it set you free
This is the journey from duality
To oneness

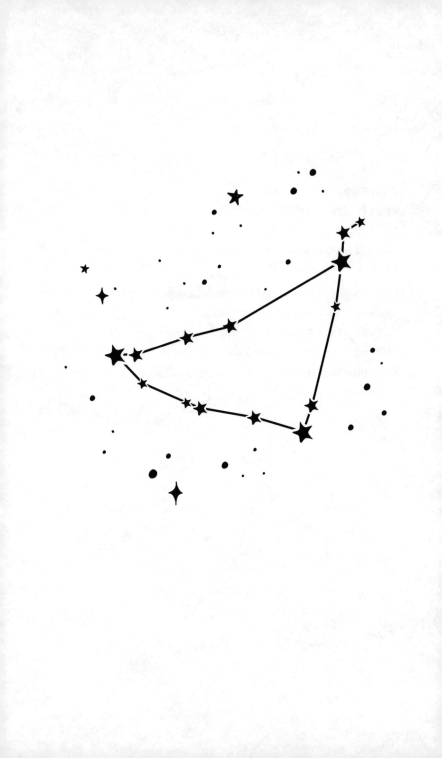

Lucid Living

Life is but a dream
Where nothing is ever as it seems
It projects our internal reality
So we can heal our diseased mentalities
Oh, how we become focused on the tiny things
When peace is never what this mindset brings
Every enlightened being knows
That they create their day
They surrender to the flow
So the universe has space to bring miracles
their way

The Guide Inside

We run around all day
Thinking this is important
This we must do
But what can be more important
Than having a sacred appointment with you?
We ask everyone's opinion
Should I do this or that?
Go inside and ask yourself!
You'll never have to look back
Only you can give yourself clarity
So why do we trust ourselves so warily?
As though another's seal of approval
Will save us from failure's grasp
If we are always trying to avoid it
We will never succeed in any task
Trust the guide inside
The one whose voice is humble and wise
And if failure steps across your path
Do not try to avoid its wrath
Instead, ask what it is here to teach
Only through learning can your dreams be reached

Love Yourself Now

If you think all you are
Is who you could be
Then you will never experience
Your own divinity

Love yourself Now:

A lot of us have an affair with this future version of ourselves
that looks a certain way and has achieved certain things,
but that completely dishonors who we are right now. So
many different lives had to be lived for us to even
be born, and no moment has been wasted in
becoming who we are right now, and so there's a grace
that comes with falling in love with the process

Seeking Truth

We all seek a universal truth
It reveals itself through nature, animals, and youth
Its song can only be heard when we slow down
Through solitude and silence, we'll finally be found

Life plays this funny game
Where we seek truth through fortune, lust, and fame
But truth has always lived within
Whispering wisdom to us in the ever-changing winds

Truth touches us in glimpses of passion
We want to believe in magic yet bury it in ration

Truth cannot be captured in words
And yet I still try, hoping I'm heard
We are blind to our own power
And enslaved to a matrix run by the clock's hour
Like a rabbit chasing a carrot, we run in circles,
Forgetting we are the Universe
Our consciousness eternal

If you are seeking a universal truth
Know that the Universe itself lives within you
All the answers exist inside
Slow down, get still, open your eyes

Phoenix Rising

Problems arise when we forget who we are
The consciousness behind our thoughts
The being made of dust from a billion-year-old star
But the path of love and creativity
Comes from finding your voice
From making even the simplest of decisions a
mindful choice
Always keep your shadow in front of you
Where you can see it
Make peace with the darkness in you
And you will find clarity beneath the mind's mist
Like a phoenix rising, you will be reborn
into the light
The strength of lessons learned laced into
your wings as you take flight

Phoenix Rising:

To be honest, the imagery of the phoenix came to me from reading Harry Potter. There is a scene when Fawkes (Dumbledore's phoenix) bursts into flames at the end of his life. Moments later he is reborn before Harry's eyes. I loved that as a visual for our growth as human beings. Except we choose whether or not to rise from the ashes.

Celestial Harmony

Honor your phases
As you would the moon
You never look up and think
"You should be this or that,"
You honor her waning
How she faces darkness
And walks through her own shadow

You honor her waxing
How she grows and expands
Shining her light as bright as possible
You never think she should stay dark for the
Sun's comfort
You honor her fullness and allow her to be wild

When she is waning again
She never fears that she will return to the light
She honors all sides of herself equally
Knowing that there is a time for shadow
And there is a time for light
All things in nature embody this balance

Celestial Harmony:

This was the first poem I wrote for this collection.
In Los Angeles, the sky was always void of
stars, but there were some nights when the moon
was so close I felt I could almost touch her.
I used to expect myself to be bright and full all
the time, but that dishonored my shadow.
Self-acceptance is learning to move with the
ebb and flow of our transformational
tides.

Lens of Experience

We all see a virtual reality
Projected through individual mentalities
To a tree whose roots run deep
The universe is only knowable through
What its branches reach
To a bird that spreads her wings
She travels the world untethered
Seeing far-off things

Some humans stay comfortable and rooted
Afraid of the unknown, their minds polluted
But for those of us who roam
The present moment is our eternal home

There is a time to flap your wings
And a time when we must root to rise
Find this balance
And you will never feel lost inside

Lens of Experience:

I lived on the north shore of Oahu, and there was this
hike in the back of the jungle near my home.
It lead to an old tree that had fallen on her

side and had thick roots that ran deep.

I would lay on her at sunrise every morning
and place myself in the perspective of the different
parts of the forest. The birds, the trees, the ants.
We can get so caught in our own perception we
forget there are many different valuable lenses to see through.

Time

A man-made law that binds us is Time
Everyone is under the illusion
That it works in a straight line

Past, present, and future exist all at once
Déjà vu is merely an intuitive hunch
It is the ghost of a lesson we have already learned
Reminding us to choose differently and discern

Have you ever felt the day move too fast?
Or feel time pass so slowly
That it seems the moment will forever last?
The clock marks how long we are alive
We think Time is killing us, but we do not
realize
We can speed Time up or slow it down
And let go of the idea that by a certain age
We will be found

Have fun in your twenties
And make a lot of money
Find that person
And settle in
Take medication to give yourself

A permanent grin
When will we wake up
And stop following what has been?

Where we are bound
Love will set us free
Untether your soul and don't let
Time tell you who you should be
Play when you're eighty
And be wise at eighteen
Create your own reality
And never lose sight of your dreams

Patience

What is patience?
It is a spiritual form of waiting
I think I'd prefer to be immersed in the now
Rather than wonder when
Things will manifest or how

Patience

I'm very impatient with myself. Especially when it
comes to the future. A mentor of mine said to me,
"you have plenty of time, but none to waste."
There is a magic that comes with learning
to love the mysterious patterns through which life
unfolds

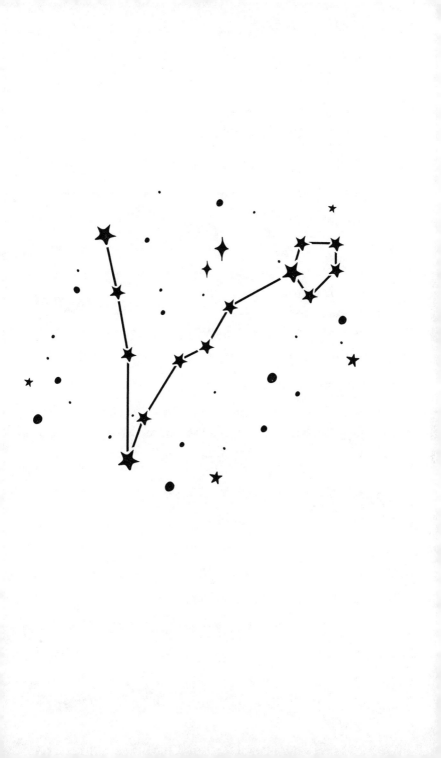

Lessons from Trauma

I am the sum of all my ancestors who came before
I have inherited their fear and anxiety
Wrapped up in traumas past worn
Not safe to have a voice, I lived silently

This was never mine to carry
It was never theirs
By facing these old traumas, I receive clarity
This ends with me and heals as I become aware

When your pain body gets triggered
Remember, "this isn't me."
As we let go of the belief that we're internally injured
We'll come home to the pure part of us that
has always been free

Lessons from Trauma

I wrote this during my craniosacral training.
We were doing a lot of work with
past trauma, and I began to notice the
same patterns I had could be traced back
through my mother and her mother.
If you really reflect on the past, you begin
to see why you are the way you are in
the present. And that's the beautiful
thing about awareness. When you
keep your shadow in front of you,
you can shine light on those darker places
that need to be loved.

Release Yourself Back to Yourself

You were once wild and untamed
This is your natural state of being
And it is where you shall return to
Remembering who you are is quite freeing
And will heal all you have been through

Maintain your purity of heart
And your dancing soul
The world will try to change you
But you are more precious than any gold

If everyone approves of you
Then it's time to give your life an upheaval
Stand your ground empowered and true
Hold nothing back
And be unapologetically you

The Guru

Listen to your parents
Your friends
Your teachers
Honor their opinions
For they provide different perspectives

Leave the final say to the guru
The guru is the one who transforms
Dark into Light
It is the one who is honest and wise
Whose voice can only be heard
In silence and stillness
The guru is you

Intrinsic Worth

Slow down, breathe, my love
There will always be
Something important to attend to
And yet, what is more important than
To sit and be in total peace?
We fear silence
Yet through silence, we are free
Prison only exists within
When we face our pain
We will no longer be held back by what has been
Slow down, breathe, my love
Listen to the voice inside
It is wise and wants you to be joyfully alive
It intends that you actualize your soul's potential
No longer living on autopilot
Or waiting for the world to hand you self-worth
In a stack of credentials
Your soul has intrinsic value
It has nothing to do with
Status, beauty, or success

Slow down, breathe, my love
Listen to the voice inside
You'll know what path to take
If you follow that inner guide

Meet Me in the Center

Give a gift to each person you meet
If you knew their whole story
You'd find none of your judgments to be concrete
For in the end, we are not so different

And all of us are equally significant
Our shells may vary in color and size
But we are connected through
Universal love inside

Give a gift to each person you meet
They have their own struggle beyond what you see
Hate does not take a break
And fear spreads like wildfire
There is too much at stake
Lives are being sacrificed for dollars and empires

Love must always be our response
The world cannot afford ignorance and nonchalance
Everything that is happening directly affects you
Just because it is not at your doorstep
Does not make it of less value

We are each responsible for spreading light
And leaving this world better
Ensuring everyone their rights

Good and evil do not exist
Pointing fingers only separates us from bliss
I will meet you in the middle of Light and Dark
Where we can stand in the center
United heart

meet me in the center

The first time I ever eye gazed was at a workshop. It's essentially what it sounds like - you stare into the eyes of a stranger for several minutes. to break down the barriers that normally exist in social settings. There was this one guy at the workshop that I judged before even knowing, but then we eye gazed for ten minutes. Both of us cried, and by the end I felt closer to him than many of my closest friends. If we all took the time to learn each others stories and connect on a deeper level, there would not be a single person undeserving of our love and compassion.

From Lonely to Alone

At first, becoming whole is lonely
We shed our old skin
And some relationships may temporarily fade away
As the uncertainty of our identities are shaken up
We become empty but not in a hollow way
In the way that space is empty and contains the
whole universe
We learn to belong to ourselves
And as our hearts become our home
We can learn to belong to the whole world
To love it in its entirety
The fear of facing ourselves is when we disconnect
And fall prey to illusions of separation
Unconditional love flows in when we are brave
enough
To face our own souls through eyes of compassion
So it can then flow out and remind every soul
That they are love itself

Purpose Beyond Perfection

I feel their eyes on me
All with their own opinions of how I should be
There is always something I should change
How do I keep my heart open?
I must stay focused in my lane

Stick to your vision
To what makes your heart soar
If you try to please everyone
You will never grow to be more

We don't need more perfect people
Sculpted by an idea that is unreachable
Be yourself and stay in your lane
If your work is true
It will see you through fear and pain

Let them see you how they please
They will praise you or judge you
Expectations impossible to meet
This was never between you and them

Follow your heart
And you will uncover the greatest gems
So many gifts hidden inside of you
The universe wants you to discover them
To know you are courageous and true

And when you find them, give these gifts to the
world
Share with your whole heart
Whether they receive it as a rock or a pearl

This has always been between you and the universe
Maintain your integrity, and you will be immersed

In the greatest love you have ever known
One that comes from inside
With an unshakeable purpose that shows you
Why you are alive

Untethered Love

People often come in and out of our lives as
messengers of light, as wonderful teachers
Each of them carrying with them a lesson
Some of them stay for a lifetime
Some of them only for a moment like a bright
comet passing by
But when we absorb the lesson we're meant to
learn from them
They continue along their way
We will always find what is meant for us
Whether we take this path or that
Different lessons all leading to the same Truth
Love respects the free will of everyone's journey
For it was never ours to command in the first place

Lessons from the Sea

Floating out in the turquoise sea
She wondered life's great mystery
Who are we, and how did we come to be?

She gazed out, observing the moonlit tides
An undiscovered ocean with a world underneath
The Sea gazed back and wondered if she'd realize
The answers are always hidden in plain view
Simple, and yet our doubt blinds us from Truth

"I could tell her everything," the Sea thought
But to be Awake this can't be taught
Many wonder, but few are brave
To pass through life's trials, their hearts untamed

Self-discovery is the key
To unlocking life's great mystery
Dive underneath the chaotic waves within
And you will discover Eternity
As it has always been

Stagnation

What do we do in times of stagnation?
Where we feel stuck and have lost inspiration?

Sometimes "it's all happening" seems a false
incantation
But remembering this truth is such a simple
salvation

We say go with the flow because life comes in waves
There are times where our lives will have too fast
a pace

There are times when our to-do list will overwhelm
And times when we will need to ask for help

There are slow waves where we won't know what to do
Where we forget our purpose and that this is
temporary too

We are gifted these times where not much is
happening
To learn the importance of connection and
tapping in
By slowing down and discovering we are more
We can live each day more empowered than before

Then return to the fast pace of life with fresh
eyes
Tapped into a deeper layer of love inside

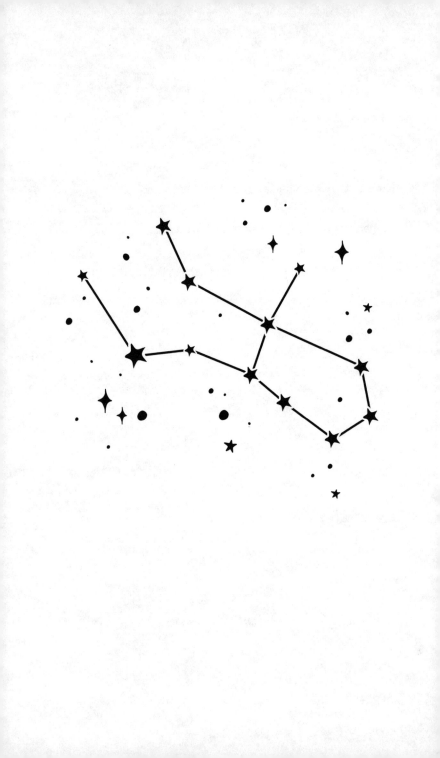

Dissolving Barriers

Who do you think you are?
It is strange how we confuse
Self-deprecation with being humble
The voice in our head loves to abuse
And bury truth beneath its harsh jumble

How do you speak about yourself?
Do you feel proud or rejoice in your inner wealth?
Do you walk down the street confident and free?
Or have you forgotten this is how we are
naturally meant to be?

Never be afraid to shine your light
Expand and take up more space than you think
is right
Recall the Wild Soul within
And know your spirit expands
Beyond your skin

Lessons from Anger

Anger is the energy of transformation
It is a volcano erupting and giving birth to an
island
Use it as a catalyst for honest contemplation
If you speak to it in the safety of silence
It will reveal what is important to you
And what you hold yourself back from
Allow the full expression of anger to come through
And harness its energy to empower the beat of your
own drum
Transform it to fuel your creative fire
Let it become the unstoppable force that manifests
your desires

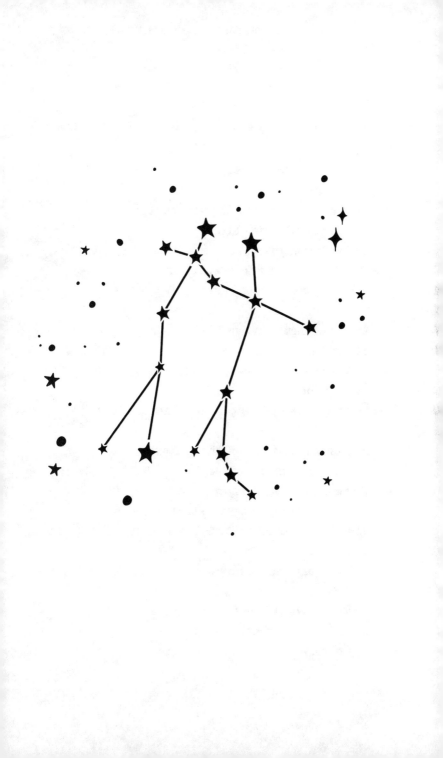

Art Awakens the Heart

Let your art be the tether
That brings you home to your heart
If you start to view life
Through a magnifying glass
Practice an art and you will see
None of your worries last

Art is alchemy, free and bold
It can turn the heaviest situation of lead
Into the wisest lesson of gold
It helps us to understand why
Through all challenges and changes of life

Art is the language of the universe
It speaks to us in drops of paint
Or in the ink of a writer's pen
It burns through any constraint
The flame of creativity is alive in us all
It is medicine for the soul
And can break down any wall

Art can take the shape of any mold
It is fluid, ever-changing
Art cannot be pinned into a hole

Look for Art's presence everywhere and you
will see
It is throughout all of nature
And the very lungs you breathe

Origins

Creativity is the pulse of our intuition
It burns through the limitations of the mind
So our dreams can come into fruition
Pleasure is how we control time
And through this immersion of presence
Our mind, body, and spirit align
To the origins of our infinite essence

Patient Pursuit

Perhaps the answer is never "no,"
But rather, "not now"
What we think we want
Is based on what we know

But perhaps what we do not know
Is that there is something much better
Already on its way
When you wish and manifest
Or when you pray
Make sure to add
"This or something better,"
Instead of getting stuck on what you crave

Be content with what is
The more gratitude you feel
The more you will attract bliss

Always be excited for what is to come
For our dreaming is never truly done
Know you are never lacking
For all things are one

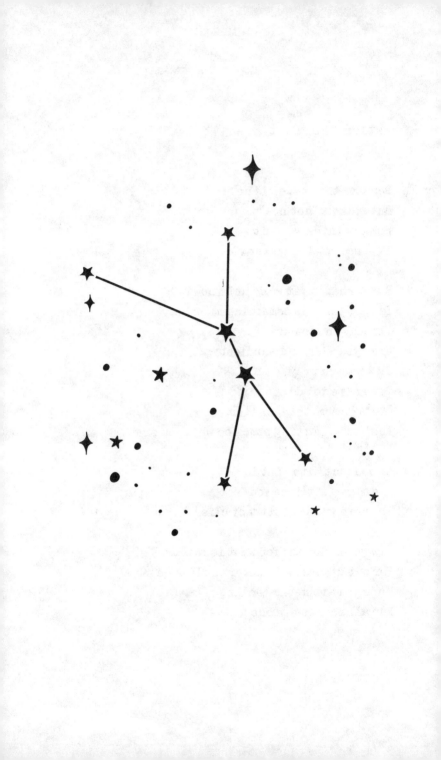

Hold Nothing Back

We receive in life
What we are bold enough
To take action with
But rejection haunts us
And prevents us
From feeling empowered by this

We have a short amount of time
On this spinning blue ball
So leap regardless of
If the net appears
You are not on this planet to crawl

Expectations

We all see through the lens of our personal
experience
No two realities the same
Too many different expectations
Impossible to maintain

How can I balance everyone's happiness
While maintaining the integrity of my heart?
I must hold strong boundaries
And see each being as a work of art

Some will trigger you, frustrate you, or upset you

But you are responsible for remembering the truth
That Spirit lives within them too
And if we are to let go of reaction
Then we must surrender the resentment behind
every action
The solution is to see through the eyes of love

For no character defect is fatal
And every alchemist is infinitely able
To mend the deepest wounds
And support every flower on their journey to
bloom

The Medicine of an Open Heart

Strength is keeping our hearts open
Instead of becoming hardened by life's trials
Insecurity will always be loud and demanding
It needs to be seen and validated constantly
Compassion is subtle
Compassion is our truest form of strength
Our power lies in empathy
Empathy provides understanding
And understanding alleviates suffering

The Lesson of Arrows

Human beings are always shooting out
imaginary arrows
That are meant to be intercepted by someone else
Depending on what we are meant to learn at that time

And when two people's arrows intercept
There is a moment that changes a person's life
Into what it is meant to be

Our arrows never miss their target
People walk into our lives with purpose
Shining light on what we need to heal
Within ourselves

The Lesson of Arrows:

When I fell in love for the first time, it felt like I had caught this invisible arrow. It came out of nowhere and aimed true to my heart. In love and in heartbreak, I have found relationships to be the greatest teacher in waking us up to what we need to heal within ourselves. It deepened me as a person more than any other experience.

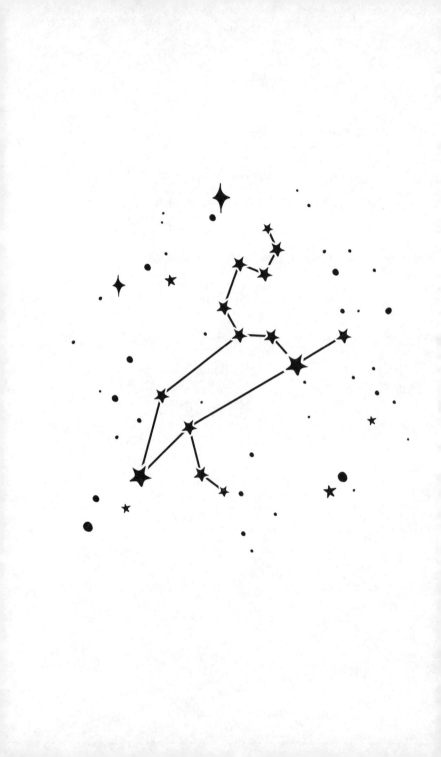

Blank Slate

I challenge you
Hit the reset button
Go a day where you let go of any ideas
About who you think you are
Who anyone else is
And what you have learned about life thus far

Walk through a day with a blank slate
Allow the world to show you a new side of itself
Let your certainty be shaken up and cracked open
You cannot become all that you are meant to be
By staying where you are

Waking up from Our Amnesia

What do we do when hope is gone?
When the light is out and we are floating along?
How do we ignite the flame within?
We are a species with amnesia
Holding on to what has been
Killing nature for instant gratification
Trading our Mother for a virtual reality to
escape in
The further away we get from truth
Chasing validation and eternal youth
Numbing ourselves in every way
Television, drugs, and phones over play

We present ourselves as a flawless mirage
Where few can see through our layered facade
How do we ignite the flame within?
By remembering we are the gods we have always
been
When one of us is hurt, all of us bleed

We must equally honor the spirit of every
flower and weed
We are souls passing through a parenthesis of
infinity
To heal the world

We must honor its divinity
Change starts with you
Heal yourself, wake up, and know this to be true
The wisdom of the cosmos dwells within you

Nature's Womb

The womb is the portal that life comes through
She moves through the birth and death of nature
In harmony with the cycles of the moon
She carries within her the wisdom of the earth
Within this masculine paradigm we have forgotten
her worth
When I speak to her and ask, "Where does it hurt?"
I feel her pain spread through every sea, city,
and desert

Natures Womb

I had always felt shame around my period,
as though it were a sign of weakness. But
giving birth is the most incredible gift
women have. Their womb is a portal
for life to come through, and that
is true strength. To experience a
death and transformation within
ourselves each month attunes women
to nature in a very special way.
Our bodies are nothing short of magic.

Conflict Creates Miracles

Do not avoid conflict
Conflict is merely energy colliding
It is nature's special way of guiding
Just like every canyon or beautiful beach
All miracles are born out of chaos
The contrast is what releases them free
There is no dream that is out of reach
This is how all things came to be
A seed never questions it will grow
Into the mightiest tree

The Way

By being tethered to past trauma
We are held captive by the mind's drama
As we remain in the present moment
We relax, and our lives continue flowing
Our breath is the password to enter peace
Through silence and stillness
We can witness our old patterns release
By shattering the mind's illusions, what is
there to gain?
We are human beings after all
Enlightenment won't protect us from pain
By remembering who we are
We stop seeking for a way and become The Way

The Mystery of Simplicity

You can search for the answers in every land
Or you can see the earth's history in a grain
of sand
The map of our ancestors laid out in the palm
of your hand
Life will reveal its secrets when we surrender
instead of demand

The Mystery of Simplicity

I took off for a year and traveled
everywhere from seeing wild elephants
in Sri Lanka, to the ~~Moroccan~~
Sahara Desert, to sand bars in
the maldives. I was looking for the
answers to a question I hadn't formed yet.
When I finally returned home, I was
playing with the sand on the beach and
began to trace it across time to when
it was once a rock, then a mountain,
and all the way back to when it was
mere stardust. I saw in the wrinkles
and lines of my hands all those
who had come before me. The
mystery unfolds all around us when
we pay attention. ~~It showeth~~
~~a spectre~~

Empowerment Within, Freedom Without

What we fear outside
Already exists within
When we heal inside
Our external fears will lose their power

Communication

Words do not just disappear into the void
Their vibrations circle the earth
They can either heal or destroy
"Be impeccable with your word"
This is a challenging thing to ask
When many people fear unfiltered honesty
And instead hide behind a sugary mask

The secret of communication
Is not in the power of words
It lies in our ability to make people feel heard
Listen with your heart
You will truly understand
You will see into their soul
And know the power of a helping hand

The River

There is a river with your name on it
With a strong current that moves
In fluidity and grace
Surrender and flow with the river of your life

If you battle upstream
You will only resist the miracles
That are on their way to you
You can never step in the same river twice
You will never again live the same moment of life

When nothing feels right
Get back into the river with your name on it
And appreciate each moment for what it is
Your job is to allow it to carry you
Without fear or resistance

Trials and challenges do not come
Because life is against you
They are wonderful teachers
That sculpt our souls

They mirror to us our strength
And when we no longer fight or play victim
The dam in our mind is removed
And the river can carry us to the next level
Until we remember we are whole

This Too Shall Pass

In the depths of depression
My mother said to me
"This too shall pass,"
For all things are temporary
And nothing truly lasts

In my highest state of ecstasy
When I was untethered and wild
My mother gave me her wisest, knowing smile
She saw into the depths of me and said
"This too shall pass,"
For all things shift and change
And this moment shall never be the same

Self-Care is Love

How do I balance a generous heart?
With the balance of self-care
Where do I start?
If we are not all equal in life's game
Then how do I remember we are all the same?
Can you treat a struggling stranger
With the same kindness as your loved one?
To burn out being of service is disingenuous
It is now that I realize self-care is truly generous
This is how we give without expectation
To stand unwavering in the strength of our own
love
And emit healing vibrations
We must create healthy boundaries
Be prepared for the universe will test them
profoundly
We cannot give what we do not have
Always balance the mind, body, soul triad
Through this unity we can heal what is broken
For when we open our eyes and see only love
Our eyes will truly be open

The Lightheartedness of Being

Sweet soul
Do not worry so much
Your life energy is precious
Do not waste it trying to figure things out
Your victory is already assured

Knowing the future would simply
Pull you from the present
You are right where you are meant to be
All other moments have led you to this door
And prepared you for this moment
May the highest version of your soul
That is ready to integrate
Live through you now
It is time, it is time

The Universe Inside

I look into your eyes
And I do not see a color
I see the entire cosmos
Reflected back to me

I see eternity in the recycled atoms
That make up the work of art
That is you

Love Beyond Illusions

Falling in love
Is a temporary vacation
From the mind's suffering

But to truly awaken
We must fall in love
With ourselves unconditionally
Before we can extend this
To another soul
Conditional love
Only tries to control
But unconditional love
Is to create value and happiness
For yourself
And remain whole

Regardless of if the other stays
This value and happiness
Cannot be taken away
True love is transcendent of labels and games
It is a way for the universe

To experience itself
In the most powerful way

Love's Mirror

You want someone to look
Into your soul
And love all that you are
Do you look into your soul
And love all that you are?

You want someone to fully accept,
Support, and care for you
Do you fully accept, support,
And care for yourself?

True love begins intrinsically
Only then can two independent flames
Come together and ignite a wildfire
To experience itself
In the most powerful way

Loves Mirror

I once asked my meditation teacher
in India about love, he said that when
people first fall in love they call it "lower samadhi,"
because you're seeing the divinity of your soul
reflected in another's eyes. But it doesn't last,
because we are merely gazing into a reflection
instead of discovering it within ourselves.

Lessons from a Tree

I would like to be a tree
Whose roots run deep
Whose branches grow tall
Those who gaze at her
Become present and enthralled

On the surface, she is beautiful
But her service to life
Is indisputable
She provides shade and a home
For all the creatures who roam

With her unconditional love
She transforms toxins
Into oxygen
From the sunlight above

Even as we cut her down
She is forgiving
For she knows
The impermanence of living
And allows her formless energy

To be recycled
As nature works in synergy

Warriors of Light

Before walking onto the battlefield
Paint a butterfly upon your shield
This is what it means to be a Warrior of Light
To shoot Love's arrow in every fight

Love is the water that cools hate's flame
Compassion is our reminder that we are all the same
Now is not the time to idly sit by
While freedom is stripped away and innocents die

Every single one of us makes a difference
Whether we realize it or not
We can no longer fall prey to ignorance

Moment to moment, we have a choice
To numb, disconnect, or use our voice
Speak your truth and speak it loud
One strong voice can change
The mind of any crowd

The earth's bleeding heart can seem
Impossible to heal
Just start at the place that feels most real
Pick a cause that feels genuine to you
And do your best to see it through

Do not be of service out of obligation
But instead show up out of love, respect, and
To raise the vibration

The Law of Attraction

Thoughts do not just disappear
They emit vibrations
Into the atmosphere

Your voice is your most powerful tool
In creating a reality set by your own rules
Speak up with what works for you
Your dreams will be successful
If you honor what is true

To apply the law of attraction
Be mindful of your intention behind every action
Speak your life into being
As though it has already happened

First, tap into your inner mystery
Visualize your dream life
As though it is already a memory
The universe responds to belief

The world will change

As you take bigger leaps
Life alters through your lens of perception
Know your worth
And practice reception

Traveling to Myself

The more places I go
The more I realize I will never
Fully understand this world
Through the eyes of logic
But when I close my eyes
And find stillness in my heart
I can feel it
It's a part of me
It's a part of you

Facing Your Soul

When we skip over our pain
And go straight to positivity
It is like floating on the surface of the ocean
Looking for a treasure that only exists in the depths
You cannot reach dawn without walking through
the night
A seed is planted in darkness before it grows
toward the light

The Golden Key

Any time another triggers you
Or hurts you
Any time you judge another
A golden key is being revealed to you

This pain is a blessing
For it is revealing the part of you that is
unhealed
So you can face your own soul
And release all that holds you back

You are not a victim of circumstance
You have called this in
Because you are ready to be more than what you
have been

The Whole is unconditional love and acceptance
Just look at any deity, master, or leader
They used every situation as a catalyst for
healing

In bringing forth even more light
Be awake to all challenges
And recognize them as a golden key
Look inside yourself

Why does this hurt?
Where does this come from?
How can we forgive ourselves and let go?

See past the mistake of another and into the
divine in them
So you can see past the pain inside you and
know the divine as yourself

Merging in the Now

Time moves within and without us
Through endless spirals
With all things merging as one
In the here and now
See eternity through
The twinkling cosmic ocean
Or hold infinity in a small seed
Whichever lens you look through
It will all lead you back to this moment

Ubuntu

Underneath it all
We crave the same thing
Love, connection, belonging
To see and be seen
To feel and be felt
If we stripped down
To the deepest motivation behind every action
We would see into our hearts' desires
And recognize the thread that connects every soul
The infinite energy that lives and breathes
through us
Is the very Love we are searching for

The Eye of the Cosmic Storm

Transcendence is achieved through the eyes of love
When we stop waiting around for a sign from above
Fate is not in charge you see
We cannot always rest on the excuse that all things
are meant to be
Though certain things are written, our hearts are
always free
Every moment we have the choice of what direction
to go in
Free Will has no compass

And if your spirit does not stop at the barrier of
your skin
Then what are the limits to where we can go?
That my love, only you will know
As you take down the barriers you have built
within your mind
As you break the bondage of societal agreements
and the laws of time

You can get to wherever you want to be from wherever
you are,
Once you remember that there was never a set bar
You are ancient atoms recycled and transformed
The secret to happiness is learning to dance in the
eye of every storm

So Hum—I Am That I Am

The moment we identify what Love is
We merely identify what it is not
If you are a seeker of Love
Do not seek the edges of the earth
Seek within
You can travel to the edges of your soul
Only to find there are none
For you are the is-ness that merges with everything

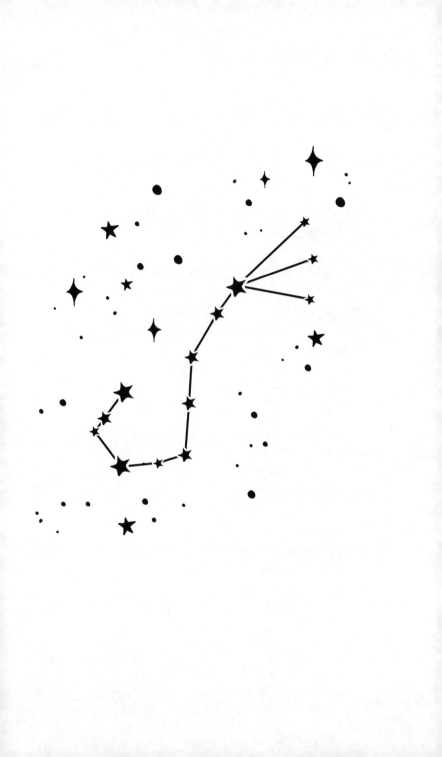

Inner Animal

A leaf came down and kissed me on the face
As I looked up, I saw a bird take flight
Its wings spread beneath the sun's rays

We spend so much of our lives looking down
Getting lost in the chatter of our minds
Or stressfully running around

As the bird flew away
I felt the warm sun kiss my skin
And imagined my own wings spreading
For in our deepest state we are akin

This bird symbolized freedom from desire
Call on the animal of your choice
Whose qualities you most admire
Get outside of yourself and away from the
mind's voice
Slip into your animal skin
For in your untamed wildness
You'll find autonomy within

Spiritual Paralysis

Knowing too much becomes spiritual paralysis
Unable to jump first and ask questions later
Experience has been squandered by over-analysis
I can map out the entire ocean for you
And tell you all its coordinates and facts
But I have yet to swim underneath the big blue
And feel a wave's impact
Knowledge crumbles on the hard shell of the mind
Until it is lived as experience in the heart
Then it can become wisdom beyond time
There are no mistakes if we learn
They become colorful stories that make up our being
Though it is important to always discern
Life is made up of courageous moments
Where we dissolve our limits
And find deeper meaning

What Does Your Life Reflect?

And I hope your choices reflect
Your dreams and not your fears
For we are the size of tiny insects
In the many galaxies of the cosmos

Do not waste your one life playing small
Feel the full range of who you are
Every moment you live
Bring the light and fire of the brightest star

And always make sure to forgive
You are meant for more than
Holding on to old scars
The most beautiful creations were born in darkness

Joined with the light of perspective and experience
Always keep creating regardless
And stay passionately curious
Wisdom is failure alchemized

Passed down to those brave enough
To take new strides
As Dark and Light intersect,
I hope boldness and bravery
Are what your life reflects

Contradictions

As living beings, we are always evolving
Our DNA itself grows and changes
We create problems to feel good about solving
And have forgotten the wisdom of the ages

This is not the age of wisdom
It is the age of information
All certainty of our belief systems
Have been cracked open and shaken

"There is one Truth," they say
Though no one seems to know what it is
Religion, science, and spirituality are all the
"right" way
Though each other they dismiss

Perhaps I contradict my beliefs
They are always shifting
And to me, this is a relief
For to believe one thing my entire life
Is to ensure that from Truth I'll be drifting

I do not trust those that stay the same
It means they are submissive
To society's complex game

It means to their heart they are dismissive
And choose security over growth

Question everything
Especially you
And to one idea, never cling
This way, you will discern what's true
To believe strongly
Limits our perception of the world
There are infinite possibilities
Beyond what the human brain
Can perceive

Beyond the Surface

Why do we always ask the same questions?
What is your name?
Where are you from?
What do you do?

This teaches us nothing about what they have
been through
We learn little about who they truly are
Their hopes and dreams or how they learned
from their scars

There is a mechanicalness in the average
conversation
We are either on autopilot or caught in our
agenda's fixation
Sometimes we ask new questions out of infatuation

We must ask better questions for the sake of
connection
Stories unite us and dissolve our fear of
rejection
Each being is a teacher and can give you a gift
A lesson that will bring you closer to finding
your bliss

Our deepest connections often come in
The form of who we least expect
They smack us awake
And show us what we need to accept

Unconditional love is the end game
It is how we heal conditioning and deep-rooted shame
So, what questions can we ask
To see through each other's masks?
Expansive questions have the power to unlock
any door
They will help us find deeper connection than before

Intertwined Yet Free

There's no place I'd rather be
Than down by the sparkling sea
It is here I dream of you and me
Our hearts intertwined, yet free

Courage is all Love asks
She prays we are up to the task
In True Love, we must take off our masks
The Source of our souls reflected back

When you see into someone's heart
And know their spirit to be pure
Recognize the universe in them
Beyond the naked eye's allure

Questions for the Cosmos

When the big bang occurred
Did time and space emerge with it?
The answers seem to be a blur
Buried beneath too many opinions

How are colors made in the universe?
Beyond refractions of light
And are we in a multiverse
With dimensions and portals alike?

How is love made in scientific terms?
Or is it unexplained, immeasurable poetry?
Is experience the only way in which we can
truly learn?
And what does it mean to be a soul that's free?

Can the power of the mind
Heal illness and transcend time?
And what are we doing here in the first place?
Is it all random and pointless, a trial of free will?

Or is it governed by destiny and fate?
I pray to these mysteries the universe will one
day spill

Until then, I shall live the questions
For I think exploring them
Is our greatest creative expression

We're human beings, after all
Both one with the universe
And yet incredibly small
We all seem to be making this up as we go

So enjoy life like a huge party
But don't forget to grow
Balance is the center of contrast
To live numbly or in ecstasy is a choice
For even the world itself won't last

Eternal Beings

Eternity slumbers in me
And She will only awaken
When I open my heart
To where She already resides
And allow her to merge with infinity

The Intersection of Life

Our stories are precious gifts
Laced with lessons
Embodying the paradox of being
Share your story with your heart and soul
It is a message for all those who listen
We did not come to know each other by accident
This sharing of time and space
When we entrust each other with our stories
A cosmic energy spirals throughout us

The Awakening

When I found home within myself
I was free
When I truly loved myself
I opened my eyes
And could finally see
I gazed at everything
And recognized it as me

The Awakening

I had this brief moment of clarity, like
poking my head above the clouds and feeling
the golden sun on my skin. I felt this overwhelming
love inside, and for the first time stopped
trying to make a person or place my home.

Home was within my very skin. I may not
always live in that place, but I
can still connect to that feeling.

Melt into Me

As we leave our minds astray
Our spirits grow beyond the Milky Way
I have never known a heart so pure
I recognize those ancient eyes
Deeper than your shell's allure
A cosmic ocean flowing inside
Energetic waves of consciousness
As you teach me to surf
My life's journey with confidence
The fears of my mind can no longer prevail
For I now see all that is not love
As an illusory tale
Our love is a flame that never burns
It merely ignites our purpose
Deepening our ability to learn

Moving Meditation

Movement is the language of feeling
Through the exploration of my body and breath
I am learning the art of being
And if the path appears everywhere that we step
Then there are no wrong turns
And we become free of regrets
Choice is merely an act of hesitation
Where we imagine all outcomes
And get lost in stagnation
Each moment shapes who we become
But our decisions are impermanent since
All things are One
Trust all is happening, and never stress over how
The only moment you'll ever arrive to is Now

Certainty vs. Mystery

The only thing that can be known
Is the unknown
Fall in love with the mystery
The universal soul cannot
be Understood through ration
It is felt in its entirety
Through the silence and stillness of Being

Freedom of Possession

Love is an infinite dance with the universe
It is a fire igniting in unspoken words
Setting aflame the dark corners within us we
had thought forgotten
Love's fire can only exist where there is oxygen
Possession extinguishes this fire, and if love
is the oxygen of life
Then we respect the will of all beings that
cross our path

Awakened Wanderlust

Oh, to dream of far-off places
Cobblestone streets and different cultural paces
The aroma of espresso, pastries, and crisp air
The sounds of celebration, movement, life
New explorations shared
Reading an old book at a little café
Writing about the characters
That walk by throughout the day
This is the traveler's way
To roam through time and space
Our perspectives constantly shifting states

Garden of Eden

Can you be present
And use your imagination at the same time?
Time itself is merely a construct of the mind
And if the imagination is the bridge
To our intuition
Then we must set ourselves free
And stop waiting for anyone else's permission
Anxiety is a waste of the imagination
Meant to keep us suffering
Follow the pull of your heart
It is your passport to freedom
Paradise dwells within
And reveals itself only when
We stop seeking an external Garden of Eden

Arrive

We have nowhere to go
Nowhere to arrive
This is an illusion
Distracting us from
The eternal wealth inside

Lessons from Pain

Crack my heart open so new light can come in
As I learn to dance with my shadow
I return to the spark of divinity I have always been
You have been my mirror and torn down my walls
I will never run from Love's pain
For if I am to become Love itself
I will embrace it entirely and never play games
I am formless form
Expanding beyond this shell
My heart and soul no longer torn
As I become free of my mind's hell

Lessons from Power

What is power?
The life force of the present that arises from within
It is the energy of love
That is beyond the sum of who we have been
What is awakening?
To still exist within time and space
But to be grounded in the truth of the present
Free of the mind's race
What is service?
Mirroring the goodness of every soul
So they too can know love's power and merge in
with the whole

Lessons from a Spider

I have roots that roam
Like a spider weaving her web
I create an infinite amount of homes
Never attached to one place I go
I surrender to the direction
The river of spirit flows

I string my own fate
On an iridescent silk thread
It is strong yet subject to change
When my masterpiece is destroyed
I do not feel dread
All things return to an infinite void
I create simply for my spirit's joy

Thought Loops

How do I still my brain's chatter
And silence any thought loops
That reinforce old patterns
The answer is not about silencing the voice at all
It can be of deep service
But it can also create walls
So I shall tell you of its purpose
But do not give it more power than this
For the voice can also create suffering
Or it can be the foundation of bliss

The brain uses itself to understand its own
existence
A miracle forgotten so easily
When we believe its illusions we create resistance
The magic of the Now overlooked ceaselessly

We are the only animals on this planet
That can decide what life to live
This too we take for granted
But the present moment always forgives

Cosmic Humor

How do I have an open heart?
In a world of such suffering
Where do I start?

In an age of skepticism and digital isolation
The antidote is creative activism
And spiritual transformation

Keep your heart open
And do not worry about rejection
For everything is a mere projection
The key to empowerment is self-acceptance

And if it's true that this is all a dream
Then our beliefs should never be taken to the
extreme
A cosmic sense of humor will help us see
That our only universal purpose is to learn
how to Be
This too we take for granted
But the present moment always forgives

The Future

What if we stopped asking,
"How will this turn out?"
And ceased wondering
If we're meant to take a certain route

What if we recognized
Our path is wherever we step?
And released feeling lost
Or caught in a wave of regret

What if we no longer
Held on to what has been?
And remembered we are Weavers of our fate
Creating a web of magic within

Masters of Fate

We are Queens and Kings
All dressed in rags
Too focused on small things
Forgetting the power we once had

Roll your shoulders back
Feel the universe you hold in your heart
Get back on your soul's path
Remember the royal you've been from the start

To be a master of your fate
Holds great responsibility
We must use it in a loving way
Empowering others to find peace

Do you remember what it was like?
When your body worked in harmony with nature
When you were tuned in to all of life?
For as we become one, our power is greater

La Luna

She lights the way
And invites you into the dark
Her iridescence cannot be seen by day
At night, she's a ruler of the stars
She controls the tides of psychic flow
And teaches us to love our darkness
So we may fully embody our inner glow
She is the seer of souls
From her eyes we cannot hide
If you seek to learn from her mystery
Be prepared to grow
And live from a deeper layer of love inside

Kali

You may know me as the destroyer
I shatter ignorance and illusion
To allow your true self to come forward
My purifying anger incinerates the mind's confusion

I am shadow wrapped in stars
I translate the wisdom of the moon
You will find me in the lessons of your scars
Though the ego I consume

I am the energy of chaos
To the brave I birth new life
Those who value comfort are forever lost
I am unapologetic in my transformational tides

What We Are Made Of

I am of the earth
My heart is the deepest part of the sea
The flowers are my lips
My eyes exist within every tree
The curve of their branches my hips
My arms are the wings of every bird
My spine forged by mountains
Through the wind, you'll hear my whispering word
My energy is always surrounding
I am the rays of the sun that warm your skin
Helping you to meet your truth within
You are of the earth
Sink into your body's wisdom
And you shall know your worth
Beyond the bondage of time or distance

Faith over Fear

Watch when your certainty is shaken
How many thoughts will flood your mind
Like fear in the form of horses racing
The illusion of control shattered in time

It is much easier to stay in the comfort of what
we know
But evolution is a trust fall
And the unknown is how we grow

We are the entire universe experiencing itself
in this form
Uncertainty is when our existence is most honest
As we bring deeper awareness to the life we explore
There is no such thing as a permanent promise
For we are only guaranteed the now
Every supernova is unpredictable yet flawless
It is in our nature to transform
And we never truly decide when or how

Conscious Connection

Look into a person's eyes
And be present for their soul
This is more healing
Than you could ever know
I honor the place in you
Where the entire universe resides
This conscious connection is why we are alive

Respect the Rose's Thorns

I am the red rose whose stem you tried to pull
And contain in a small vase of your fear
Instead, my roots grew deeper and my thorns full
For all that you are has become clear
I am the ocean you tried to contain in a drop
But my tides have only grown more wild
I have met the truth inside myself and can no
longer be stopped
Through your lessons my heart and I have
reconciled

Belonging

When you belong to yourself
You belong to the world
You can access the wisdom of every cell
If you're first willing to be unnerved
We often ask why the ground beneath us is
being shaken
Not realizing that surrendered uncertainty
Is what guides us to awaken

It Is Time

Women, it is time
Nothing is more unstoppable
Than when a Goddess decides to rise
Her magic is the kind that makes moving
mountains possible

Men, it is time
For you to know your true power
Not what you have felt in this paradigm
But instead what it is to live vulnerably
By crumbling the protective walls you built in
your heart's tower

We are so much more than our minds can comprehend
The synergy of masculine and feminine
Reveals our oneness as it has always been
Through this truth the duality of human nature
can begin to transcend

Letter from the Author

When I originally released *Explorations of a Cosmic Soul*, I desperately wanted answers to questions that have been asked since the beginning: Who are we really? Why are we here? What's the point? Since then, I have come to understand that seeking answers is a form of control, a way of gripping life tightly with white knuckles and begging for a sense of security and comfort. Yet, if we can find security within insecurity and comfort within discomfort, then life opens to us. Suddenly we take the unknown's hand and start dancing with the mystery.

Through this process, everything becomes sacred because we have our finger on the pulse of how temporary and rare life is.

When I look back on this book, I see my growth as an artist but also as a soul. A lot of the poems I originally wrote here were merely ideologies for me— concepts I was exploring but hadn't lived yet. I've learned that in order to truly affect and touch people, we have to write from our own authentic experiences because vulnerability is the birthplace of connection.

I added new poems with the hope that it empowers you to not wait for the "right time" to release your art. To get your hands dirty digging deep inside of yourself and seeing what gems you uncover.

As artists, I believe we're meant to always be emptying our creative well, so there's space for new ideas to come through. It may sound cheesy, but I believe everyone is a poet. It's just whether or not you've put pen to paper and exercised that muscle.

If there's one thing you take from this collection, I hope it's to live the questions more. To trust that every experience is merely seasoning and sculpting your soul. And most importantly, that you came here as a passenger on this planet to explore. To *live*.

h u m a n

bow to your struggles they
are the boiling water
that turns your heart tender
they are the fire that forges
you into a blade of truth
they are the harsh winds
that crumble all falsehoods
they are the earth grounding you
in what it really means to be
                    h
                    u
                    m
                    a
                    n

A Daily Prayer.

Once a day, may my worldview be shattered so
that I may never grip too tightly to any one
idea. May the glass walls that encase my mind
crumble as my perspective expands. May life
soften me, deepen me, and make me more honest
than yesterday. May I live with a heart so
tender I can truly feel the world. May my love
be malleable and formless like water, able to
envelop everyone and let them feel free from
the weight of living for a while. May I make art
that is true, not for the result, but to awaken
my soul.

The Right Choice.

i will tell you the secret
to never worrying about
making the "right choice" again
if it is done from love
it will be done rightly
so why don't we just take those reins
and pass them to the heart for a while
she's been aching to be let out
of those caged ribs

The Painter

i heard Love laughing
at all of my plans
that i thought were so grand
she saw me hunched over
my life's canvas
painting with white knuckles
only creating more struggle
i finally turned to her
hair messy and eyes wild
in a frenzy of my own worries
she smiled and said,
"when will you realize
you were meant to be the paintbrush
not the painter?"
and so i surrendered my body
into Love's hands
and let her use me
so the real masterpiece could begin

Wild Things

as soon as i stopped searching
for stable ground
i discovered i had wings
grounding into groundlessness
is the way of wild things

Intuition > Advice

when you're asking everyone
what they think you should do
that is the time
to close your mouth
open your ears
and listen to the truth
the soul has been softly
whispering to you
since the beginning

fear and discomfort

are the wings that carry us
closer to truth?
strip away those
heavy layers of illusion
that weigh you down
pain is a great teacher
that leaves once she
has taught us what we need to know

The Real Guru

when you go in search of a master
life will send a thousand jokers dressed as gurus
in a crowd of preachers shouting the answers
you'll find the real one hidden in the corner
laughing at this circus of illusions

Love

Love listens to the footsteps of an ant equally
as much as the cries that come from the bottom
of your soul
and Love honors the timelessness of a grain
of sand equally as much as the timing of your
deepest desires and Love never asks the
question of your worthiness just as she never
asks if dawn will break that day
Love is life's fulfillment of itself
and she is realized through the experiences of
your heart there will be a moment when you
come to know Her
as intimately as you do the oxygen that
sustains you but until you let Her in
she will keep whispering that divine invitation
through your every experience:
surrender
surrender
surrender

take the first step.

be the one who says "i love you" first, even if
it is with a shaking voice and a thundering
heart. take the first step. be the one who
surrenders their sword of defense and meets
conflict with compassion. take the first
step. be the one who admits to their pain
before throwing up thick, cold walls. take
the first step. be the one who is direct and
honest instead of speaking behind the back
of another. take the first step. be the one
who asks for help and gives it without any
thoughts of debt. take the first step. be the one
who does not enforce their own truth, because
they know there are many truths. take the first
step. because the pain of a bruised, open heart
is far better than the pain of a closed-off one
that never knows true connection.

Mirror of Shadows

the only way to see myself
is to look at the reflection inside
there, i found a mirror of shadows
meant to test the strength of the soul
it reflected every piece of me
i had not made peace with
that kept me from becoming whole
the looking glass showed me the worst
all those messy and unlovable parts
the ways in which i hurt and was hurt
but contrast is required in any work of art
those who love honestly
are never dishonest with themselves
they do not expect to live flawlessly
for perfection is its own kind of hell
i recognize those who looked into the mirror
by the twinkle of humor in their eyes
they are the ones who were brave enough to heal
and remember all that is not love is a lie

Approval

it doesn't matter how they see you
how do you see you?
would you deny becoming
who you are meant to be
for the approval of others?
who you truly are
is far more interesting
than who anyone wishes you to be

Passion

It is not what we do
But the heart we do it with
If you are to hold power
Hold it with the same tenderness
You would a newborn
If you are to indulge
Let it be the indulgence of a heart
That knows no edges
If you are to seek love
Seek not only its beauty
But to be remolded by its brokenness
True love transforms
True indulgence is an act of surrender
True power is held by the humblest hands

The Key

all you are avoiding
is what will set you free
if you would only remember
it is you who holds the key

The Escape

human beings are rarely without an escape
plan. any situation we walk into, we need to
know the exit doors. there is only one exit, and
that is death. perhaps on the other side of
that is more life, and so the great wheel of
eternity keeps turning. we've made distraction
an exit door, a grand escape from suffering.
it makes for an apathetic world, but feelings
emerge from the infinite intelligence of our
body. they are not illogical or something to
avoid. they are the soul yelling at us, saying,
"go this way! not that way!" to be fully alive,
fully aware, and just let the world rush in with
complete acceptance is the most honest thing we
can do.

What's so funny?

when all is spinning out of control
the only sensible thing to do
is laugh louder than god
until she calms this chaotic world
just to hear what's so funny

Time.

"What about time?" he asked.
"If you choose to enter the current of linear
time, the world of the mind, do not drown in its
rapid waters. There won't be a moment's peace,
nor a flicker of stillness. All you can do is
let the river of time carry you. If you fight
its currents, the stress will kill you slowly,
and you will never enjoy life as it was meant
to be enjoyed." She paused for a moment, then
smiled and said, "But if you should greet
time as an old friend and worship only the
moment you're in, life will become a grand
celebration. The earth will be happy to kiss
your dancing feet.
You will finally know peace as your heart
stretches so big it envelops the whole world.
You will merge with the whole of life, tapping
into all there ever was, is, and will be."

"but do you feel free?"

the level to which
we are conditioned
is the level to which
we are free
every time we protect
ourselves from pain
our walls only grow taller
imprisoning our soft heart
until we can no longer
feel the world
every tragedy
becomes a distant event
that doesn't concern us
every joy becomes fleeting
and cut off by numbness
Love says
"my heart is with your heart
I will walk with you
through the dark night
of your soul."
when you think
your life is falling apart
remember it is
merely those walls
around your heart crumbling
so that more love can rush in

One Breath

This life is but one breath in Eternity's vast,
endless lungs
She buried a treasure more precious than any gold
Knowing we would spend that one breath seeking
every corner of the earth to find it
But she hid it in the one place
We'd never think to look
I'll give you a hint:
Turn your gaze within

House of Fear

Burn down every brick in that house of
fear until there is nothing left between
you and the sky. Be someone who says, "Turn
up the volume on who you are, for I have
longed to dance to your soul's song all my
life." Be someone who, when they do experience
loss, celebrates their heart for caring
instead of cursing it for crumbling. And
never again walk into a situation trying
not to get hurt, for every experience burns
away the hard shell that encloses your
heart. The path to finding freedom is the
path to following our fear—and then letting
it melt under the heat of love's embers.

Instrument of Love

I do not want to be the painter
But the paintbrush
I do not want to the musician
But the instrument
I do not want to be a writer
But the pen that is used to bleed words
So tender and honest
I want to be an instrument of love
For every atom and cell to be used

do not tell me of who you know

or what you have done
tell me of the vision you keep tucked away in
the darkest corner of your heart
that dreams so big it scares you to even peek at
it is your heart's only obligation, you know
not all this other nonsense and distraction
you spend your precious energy on
why push your dream off for "someday"
and confuse what keeps you busy with what is
important?

The Pathless Path

It's never going to work out the way you
thought it would. You can make your plans
for someday, but to walk a known path is to
die before death. We tuck away the hard truths
in the back of our hearts. That we'll die
someday. That the people we love will die. That
we'll suffer. But if we learned to bring
those fears to the forefront, if we stopped
grasping so desperately for only the highs in
life, we would actually experience more joy
than ever. It would be the joy of a soul that
welcomes every experience with open and
loving arms because there is nothing in
existence that is not sacred.

An Empty Scale.

have you convinced yourself
you are what you do?
sit in silence for ten days
and worthiness will never
be a question you ask again
have you convinced yourself
you are what people say you are?
spark a match to your reputation
and dance around the flames
of their praise and blame
have you convinced yourself
you are what you have?
give up what you own
until nothing owns you
even your body
is a borrowed sanctuary
let's smash that silly scale
you've been measuring your worth with
beneath our dancing feet
the best way to deal with
our friend called fear
is to call his bluff

Interlude

Life has no beginning
And no end
If our birth is springtime
Then death is merely
The season of winter
A temporary interlude
For the soul to rest
Before it slips into character again
We're all just here
In timeless space
Each life a chapter
Of the greatest love story ever told
How beautiful it is
To be a pen in eternity's hand for a while

Acknowledgments

I would like to thank the following people for their inspiration and encouragement . . .

My mother, who is a living example of courage and unapologetically herself. She truly understands the art of deep listening. I wouldn't be on this strange, wonderful journey called life without her.

Alexis, my sister, there are no words for what you are to me. Thank you for always helping me find the joy and humor in every situation.

My dad, who is the smartest man I know. His quiet wisdom is something I will spend a lifetime learning from.

Alexandra Gallagher, thank you for traveling the world with me and being one of the first people to read this. I'm so inspired by your grace and kindness.

Deanna Ainsworth, thank you for believing in the 18-year-old girl that walked into your yoga studio trying to find herself. You are one of the most selfless people I have ever met.

Angelica Singh, without your craniosacral training, I never would have learned to face my shadow. Thank you for helping me experience embodiment.

Jade Alectra, thank you for igniting a fire in all of our hearts and always lighting the way.

Dakota Adan, thank you for always being my dance partner and inspiring me to write and live more honestly.

Jill Wintersteen, you are a goddess. An alchemist. Your vulnerability inspires me and having your energy in this book is an honor.

Rebecca Reitz, you brought the formless into form with this cover. The way you combine your intuition with your art is unique and very needed in this world. Thank you for everything.

To the cosmic souls who have crossed my path whether virtually or in person, there are no words to express the honor it is to be a passenger on this planet with you. Thank you for showing me the value of community.

Photo credit: Rachel Anne Ray

About the Author

Allie Michelle is a poet, writer, and breathwork teacher. Her two poetry collections, *Explorations of a Cosmic Soul* and *The Rose That Blooms in the Night*, have touched millions of hearts all over the world, inspiring people to find the strength it takes to be soft. She has recently launched her online community, The Mystery School, which focuses on empowering people through holistic tools like yoga, breathwork, and meditation. Her passion for health and wellness has largely influenced her writing; Allie continues to give voice and touch the hearts of a new generation of poets and artists online, leading a community of dreamers over half a million strong.

Instagram: @alliemichellel
Website: www.themysteryschool.io

★✦.
NOTES

_____

_____

_____

_____

_____

_____

_____

_____

_____

_____

_____

_____